BREAKING
THE CYCLE

CONTENTS

Chapter 1: Breaking the Cycle

"Do the best you can until you know better. Then when you know better, do better." –
Maya Angelou

Let's get one thing straight: success in life doesn't include blaming people. It's about looking at the patterns we've been stuck in for way too long—and deciding to break free. That's why this book is called Breaking the Cycle. Because some of us are walking through life carrying stuff that was never ours to carry in the first place.

Some people inherit money, land, or grandma's famous mac and cheese recipe.

Others inherit trauma, survival skills, and the silent rule that says, "We don't talk about emotions in this house." Some people carry those negative thoughts all the way through their teenage years and into adulthood.

This book is for everybody, but I have to be real about my own story—and mine starts with slavery. My roots trace back from Nigeria to the slave ports of the Carolinas. That's where things started falling apart for my family tree. If you've ever felt like your family was holding on by a thread, you're not alone—and the thread might be way older than you think.

When our ancestors were taken from Africa, they weren't just taken from their land. They were taken from their names, their language, their culture… and most of all, their families. People were bought and sold like property. Moms were separated from their babies. Husbands were forced to watch their wives be hurt and couldn't do a thing about it. Men were punished publicly to scare everyone else into silence. The whole idea of love, safety, and family got flipped upside down.

And somehow… they survived. But survival came at a cost.

That kind of pain doesn't disappear. It passes down like a family secret no one ever talks about—but everyone feels. You might not even realize it's there, but it shows up in different ways. In anger. In fear. In silence. In parenting. In how we treat ourselves. That's what I mean by a "cycle." It's not a one-time thing. It repeats until someone says, "Enough."

Our people carried so much. And now, with all the tools we have—therapy, community, books, support groups—we owe it to them and ourselves to stop just surviving and start healing.

Let's keep it 100: If you're confused, hurt, angry, or numb, how can you be your best for someone else? You can't fix a car with broken tools. (And if you try, you'll probably just make things worse. Ask me how I know.)

That's why before we try to help others, we need to understand our own story. Do you have any pain in your heart? If you do, where did the pain begin? How did it get passed down? What are you still holding that isn't your responsibility to hold?

Sometimes, kids act out and people are quick to call them "bad." But most of the time, that kid is just hurt and doesn't know how to say it. Instead of asking what's wrong, we should be asking, "What happened?"

It's too easy to slap labels on kids. But labeling without understanding is lazy. Kids need love, patience, and people who won't give up on them.

When I had kids, I wanted my home to be a place where my kids and their friends could feel safe. No fear, no judgment—just freedom to be kids. I dreamed of a space where they could run, laugh, imagine, and make up silly games that only made sense to them.

Because if kids don't get safety at home or school, they'll look for it somewhere else. And that "somewhere else" isn't always safe.

Pain doesn't stay in one place. If it's not healed, it spills out—into schools, communities, friendships, and relationships. A hurt kid becomes a hurt adult who raises more hurt kids. That's the cycle we're here to break.

Take the song Brenda's Got a Baby by Tupac. Brenda was twelve. Her parents were deep in addiction. She was abused by someone in her family. She had no one. She ended up pregnant, alone, and eventually died. That wasn't just a sad story—it was a whole system that failed her. Her family, her neighborhood, her community. She never had a real chance.

And real life? It's full of Brendas.

My husband and I once volunteered to teach a special class at an alternative school. Usually, five students showed up. That day, only two came. I decided to sit with them, just to talk. And what they told me? Whew!

One 14-year-old girl showed me the cuts on her arms. She said self-harm and sex were the only things that numbed her pain. She found out she had herpes after the last guy lied about using a condom. Her mom and grandma were both teen moms, caught in their own battles. Who was teaching her to break the cycle?

Then there was a 16-year-old boy. When I asked what he remembered most from his childhood, he said, "Watching my dad hurt someone. And the person died." He said it like he was describing breakfast. No emotion. Nothing. His mom let him have sex at home "because at least she knows where he is." He was smoking weed by age twelve. Someone laced it. He got addicted and was in rehab by thirteen.

That's what the cycle looks like when no one steps in.

We tried to be that someone. My husband and I fostered teens—hardest age group, most overlooked. We adopted one. His grades were awful, especially in English. Every adult said he needed to be in special ed.

We said, "He doesn't need labels. He needs support."

They rolled their eyes at us. But guess what? A few months later, his report card showed Bs and Cs. No miracle. Just someone who believed in him. But healing isn't always a straight line. He backslid—hard. Started stealing, hurting the dog, messing with the younger kids. We had to place him in a facility. It broke our hearts, but he was hurting too deeply to accept love. He had to choose healing for himself. We still love him. That never changed.

Let's be real. Your parents might just trying to survive. Some are young, broken, tired, or stuck in denial.

We need to lift the shame and masks off. You matter. You belong. You have a future bigger than this pain.

And we can't do it alone.

Trying to heal yourself is hard. It's exhausting. But when we all do a little, no one gets crushed by the weight.

So let's do the work. Let's ask the hard questions. Let's listen, really listen, to the answers. Let's stop pretending like we're fine when we're not.

Breaking the cycle means changing how we talk, how we listen. It means choosing healing, even when it's messy. Even when it hurts. Even when people don't understand.

And let me warn you—some of the people who won't understand might be the ones closest to you. That's part of it too. But keep going.

We can't fix everything today. But we can start the change. We can plant new seeds. We can create a life that's not about surviving pain—but building something beautiful in spite of it.

You ready? Let's go.

OFF THE RECORD

Use these pages to write your private thoughts off the record, you don't have to share them with anyone if you don't want to!

Chapter 2: Growing Up Broke

"If poverty is a disease that infects the entire community in the
form of unemployment and violence, failing schools and broken
homes, then we can't just treat those symptoms in isolation.
We have to heal that entire community."
— President Barack Obama

Let's be real: growing up broke is a whole experience.

I'm talking about the kind of broke where ten people are squished into a tiny two-bedroom house with no insulation in the walls—just sweat, mold, and a funky smell that no amount of bleach could fix. That was my everyday reality. And trust me, bleach was used. A lot. Still, the mold won. And so did the smell. I got teased at school for it. Some kids even said I "smelled weird." On top of that, I stuttered. And if that wasn't enough, I wore clothes that were basically "fashion flashbacks"—five years out of date and handed down so many times they deserved their own family tree.

I remember being so hyped to finally get a pair of Cross Colours pants. I thought I was killin' it… until I walked into school and got roasted. Hard. That day, something shifted. I stopped trying to fit in with smiles—I started fighting instead. Swing first, deal with feelings later. That became my defense plan.

But even when I was angry, deep down I still wanted to belong. I wanted to feel normal. So I joined the basketball team and track team.

My coaches said I had real potential. My honorary big sis Cynthia even called me "Flo Jo" (look her up—legend). I started to feel like maybe I had something special.

Then came the track meet.

There I was, mid-race, running as fast as I could in my LA Gear "Michael Jackson" high-tops. Yeah… those were definitely not track shoes. They were black and silver and absolutely not meant for sprinting. But they were all I had. They were hand-me-downs, like everything else.

People in the bleachers started laughing.

I got embarrassed—so embarrassed I faked a knee injury and quit the race. Angry and humiliated, I went over to confront the kids who laughed at me. I didn't fight them, but I made sure they knew I wasn't someone to mess with. I left the team after that. I told my mom I just didn't like track anymore, but the truth was—I was tired of feeling like I didn't belong.

Here's the thing I didn't realize back then: even with the wrong shoes, I was in third or fourth place out of eight runners. If I'd kept going—if I'd had the right gear—who knows what could've happened? Maybe scholarships. Maybe big opportunities. Instead, I let shame and anger stop me. And those kids? They didn't need to swing—they still won, because I gave up.

Money was always tight at home. Like, lights getting cut off and nothing-but-condiments-in-the-fridge kind of tight. Sometimes, all we had was the free lunch at school. And when we ran out of food, Mom gave us her share so we wouldn't go hungry. I'll never forget packing syrup sandwiches for lunch one day and pretending that was all I wanted, just so no one would feel sorry for me. It was easier to pretend than to explain.

My mom worked two, sometimes three jobs. She didn't have a degree, so minimum wage was her reality. Too broke to make ends meet, but somehow still "too rich" to get government help. It made no sense.

She worked nonstop. That meant I had a lot of time on my hands. Too much. I started hanging out with kids who were always in trouble. I got in a ton of fights. Once, a guy pulled a knife on me—and I wasn't even scared. That's how numb I'd gotten. I ended up fighting him, took the knife, and walked away thinking I was invincible. That same guy? He went to prison for murder not long after. That could've been me, locked up or worse.

There were times I snapped and hurt people who didn't even deserve it. One time, I attacked a kid who was actually trying to break up a fight. I just… saw red. I was full of rage and didn't know how to deal with it. I've tried to find him since, just to apologize. That's how much it haunts me.

With no summer camps or after-school stuff (because who could afford that?), I was out doing what I wanted. One girl I hung out with had a kind of quiet energy—my mom didn't like me going to her place. Said something didn't feel right about the neighborhood. And yeah, gang violence was a real thing where we lived. But I went anyway. I just wanted to chill and feel normal.

That afternoon, we were just watching TV and laughing. That's it. Nothing wild. A few hours later, I was home, and we heard sirens. My mom and I stepped outside, and we found out that my friend had been shot—hit in the head during a drive-by while she was watching TV. She was twelve years old. And I had just been at her house.

I didn't tell my mom right away. I was scared. When I finally did, she just held me and cried. She didn't say, "I told you so" right away. She said it later—but after she made sure I knew how glad she was that I was still alive.

Even with everything we were going through, my mom never stopped trying. She warned me about the people I was hanging out with. She worked hard, she worried, she showed up. I didn't get it then, but now? Now I do.

There's more. And this part is hard to say.

When I was around 15, I started inviting people over to our house while my mom was working. I wanted to be cool. I wanted people to like me. But that led to something I never saw coming—I was touched inappropriately. Twice.

I didn't feel like I could talk to anyone. My real dad was out of the picture. My stepdad was gone too. I just… kept it inside. My mom did the best she could, but I didn't know how to tell her. I felt alone. Completely alone.

Eventually, my mom and stepdad split up. Things didn't magically get better. We used candles for light and borrowed water in jugs from the neighbors. My mom wouldn't ask for help. She was too proud. She didn't want people to know how bad it was. We eventually went to live with my uncle and aunt for a while.

Looking back, I see how hard she fought. And I see how hard I fought too—just to survive.

I got my first job at 15 to help out, working at a catfish place. I started paying for my own stuff because I didn't want to add to the stress at home. Years later, my uncle told me how much it hurt him to realize what we were going through and how he wished we'd asked for help. But we didn't. Pride can be heavy like that.

So yeah, growing up broke wasn't just about money. It was about everything that came with it—shame, silence, survival, and trying to find your place in a world that sometimes felt like it didn't care.

But here's what I want you to know: If you're struggling right now, it doesn't have to be your forever. If your family's been stuck in the same pattern for years, that doesn't mean you have to be. You can break the cycle.

You don't have to fight people just to feel seen. You don't have to stay angry just because it's what you're used to. You don't have to repeat what you came from.

Your story is still being written. And you get to hold the pen.

OFF THE RECORD

Use these pages to write your private thoughts off the record, you don't have to share them with anyone if you don't want to!

Chapter 3: Home Isn't Always Easy

When you hear the word "home," you might think of warm meals, people who love you, and a place where you can be yourself. That's what home *should* be. But for some of us, "home" hasn't always felt safe or peaceful. And if that's your reality, I want you to know this right now: it's not your fault, and you are not alone.

Let's talk honestly—without shame, without fear.

Some people grow up in homes where there's yelling, slamming doors, silence that feels heavier than a backpack full of bricks, or even worse, physical violence. When the people who are supposed to protect you are also the ones causing pain, it can feel like you're stuck in the middle of a storm with no umbrella. But here's the truth: you are not powerless. And your story does not end with the pain you've seen.

This chapter is about breaking that cycle—just like the title of this book says. It's about learning that even if your home feels broken, you don't have to stay broken with it. You can heal. You can grow. And you can become the kind of person who builds something better.

What Does "Broken Home" Even Mean?

Let's start by defining something.

A "broken home" doesn't just mean your parents are divorced. Lots of people have divorced parents and still grow up with love, support, and stability. A home feels broken when the people in it aren't working together—when love turns into control, trust turns into fear, and kids end up feeling like they're walking on eggshells.

Maybe the grown-ups in your house argue all the time, or maybe one of them has a bad temper and takes it out on everyone else. Maybe you've seen stuff that made you scared, confused, or like you had to grow up faster than you were ready for.

None of this makes *you* broken. It just means you've been carrying more than your fair share. And it's okay to admit that it's heavy.

What You See Isn't Always What You'll Be

Let's say you've grown up seeing adults yell or fight. Or maybe one person in your house uses fear to control others—slamming cabinets, raising their voice, or threatening to leave. That kind of environment makes you feel like you have to tiptoe around your own home. It's exhausting.

Now, here's something important: just because you saw this growing up doesn't mean it has to be your future.

Sometimes people think, "Well, my parents fought like this, so I guess that's just how relationships work." No, it's not. Love shouldn't hurt. Respect doesn't require fear. And yelling isn't the same as communication.

You get to decide what your future looks like. You can learn from what you saw and say, "I want something different."

It's Not Your Fault

If you only take one thing from this chapter, let it be this: whatever happened in your home is not your fault.

Grown-ups are supposed to take care of kids—not the other way around. If you ever found yourself trying to protect a sibling, comfort a parent, or avoid someone's bad mood like it was a game of emotional dodgeball, that's not okay—but it's also not your fault.

Kids sometimes think if they were better—quieter, smarter, stronger—things would've been different at home. But listen: the choices adults make are theirs. You didn't cause it. You couldn't have stopped it. And you didn't deserve it.

Finding Safe Spaces

When home doesn't feel safe, it's important to find safe spaces elsewhere. That might be:

- A friend's house where things are calm
- A trusted teacher or school counselor
- An after-school club or team
- A library, a park, or even a corner in your room where you can breathe

Sometimes, your safe space isn't even a place—it's a person. Maybe it's a coach, a cousin, or a neighbor who listens without judging. Whoever it is, hold onto them. Let them know when things feel hard. You don't have to go through this alone.

Anger Isn't the Enemy—Silence Is

Let's talk about feelings. If you've come from a home that's full of chaos, you might feel a lot of anger. And guess what? That's okay.

Anger isn't bad. It's a sign that something matters to you. What matters is how you use it.

Some people take their anger out on others because it feels easier than sitting with sadness. Some stay silent, bottling up their feelings until they explode. But you have another option: expression.

- Write about it.
- Draw it.
- Talk to someone.
- Run it out on a track.
- Scream into your pillow if you have to.

Don't let silence win. Your voice matters.

What Healing Looks Like

Healing doesn't always look like a perfect Instagram post. It looks like:

- Learning how to say how you feel without exploding
- Asking for help when you used to shut down
- Crying and not feeling ashamed about it
- Setting boundaries with people who make you feel small
- Realizing that you don't need to repeat the past

Healing doesn't mean forgetting what happened. It means refusing to let it define you.

You're allowed to feel sad. You're allowed to be angry. You're also allowed to dream, to laugh, and to want more. That's part of healing too.

Here's where it gets powerful.

You have the chance to build a different kind of life. One that isn't built on fear or control. One that feels calm, kind, and supportive—even if that's not what you had growing up.

Let's be clear: you don't have to be perfect to build this life. You don't need all the answers right now. All you need is a decision. A decision to do better with what you've been given.

Start small:

- Learn what healthy friendships look like.
- Respect yourself.
- Apologize when you mess up.
- Walk away from people who bring chaos.
- Talk to people who lift you up.

And if you need to talk to a professional—a therapist, counselor, or mentor—that's not weakness. That's wisdom. Getting help is like putting on armor before battle.

It's okay to love people who hurt you—from a distance

This one might hit hard: sometimes the people who hurt you are the same ones who raised you or people who are close to you. It might even be people you lover dearly.

That's what makes it complicated. You might love them and be mad at them at the same time. You might feel guilty for being angry. That's all normal.

Loving someone doesn't mean letting them keep hurting you. You're allowed to care from a distance. You're allowed to protect your peace. You're allowed to say, "I love you, but I need space."

You don't have to cut people off forever to break the cycle. But you do have to decide where your limits are—and stick to them. Your job is protect yourself. Reach out to a teacher or any trusted adult and be brave enough to let them help you escape.

What Real Love Looks Like

When you haven't seen healthy love up close, it can be hard to know what it even *looks* like. So here's a quick guide:

Real love is:

- Safe, not scary
- Encouraging, not controlling
- Honest, not hurtful
- Consistent, not hot-and-cold
- Patient, not pushy
- Never physically or sexually harms you.

Real love is when someone makes you feel like you can breathe easier, not like you're waiting for the next explosion.

You deserve that kind of love.

Write Your Own Ending

Your life is not a story that someone else gets to write. You hold can be the author now.

Yes, you might've grown up in a house where people fought, yelled, or made you feel invisible. But that doesn't mean you have to stay stuck in that story.

You can choose peace over violence.

You can choose kindness over anger.

You can choose healing over hurt.

You can choose *you* over an abuser.

Imagine your future. Not what people told you it would be, but what *you* want it to be. You can go to college. Or start a business. Or be a teacher, an artist, an engineer, a therapist. You can be the first in your family to change the pattern. And you will inspire others to do the same.

One Last Thing…

If your home has been hard, I want to say something that maybe no one's said to you yet: I see you. I believe you. And I'm proud of how far you've come.

You've survived things no kid should have to deal with. You've made it to today—and that means you have a future worth building.

No one gets to decide your future except you.

So keep going. Keep dreaming. Keep choosing to be the kind of person this world needs.

And when things get hard—and they will—remember this:

You are not what happened to you. You are what you decide to become next. And you're already on your way.

OFF THE RECORD

Use these pages to write your private thoughts off the record, you don't have to share them with anyone if you don't want to!

HOME ISN'T
ALWAYS EASY

Chapter 4: Heavy Thoughts

Some days feel heavier than others. Not just because of homework, drama at school, or pressure from parents—but because of something deeper. Something that sits in your chest like a rock you can't quite shake.

If you've ever felt like the world is too loud, too confusing, too *much*—you're not alone.

Mental health is just as important as physical health. And just like a cold or a broken arm, when something's not right in your mind or heart, it deserves care. It deserves attention. And most of all, *you* deserve support.

Let's talk about it. All of it. Because this is what mental health is all about.

Mental health is the way your brain and heart feel about life, about others, and about yourself. It's how you handle stress, relationships, and big emotions. Everyone has mental health—just like everyone has physical health.

Good mental health doesn't mean you're happy 24/7. It just means you're able to handle the ups and downs in healthy ways. And when that feels impossible? That's when help is needed—not because you're weak, but because you're human.

Let's be honest. Being a teenager or a pre-teen today is hard. Social media, family expectations, friend drama, grades, body image, figuring out who you are—it's a lot. And sometimes that pressure builds up.

When that pressure turns into sadness that won't go away, or stress that makes you feel stuck, it's a sign that your mental health needs attention.

You might:

- Feel down for days at a time
- Start skipping things you used to enjoy
- Want to sleep all the time—or not at all
- Feel easily irritated or angry
- Cry and not know why
- Start feeling numb, like nothing matters

These feelings are more common than you think. They don't mean you're broken. They mean you need support.

Let's Talk About Self-Harm

This part is serious, so let's take a deep breath together.

Some people—kids, teens, even adults—hurt themselves on purpose. This is called self-harm. It doesn't always mean someone wants to die. Often, it's a way to cope when emotions feel too big, too loud, or too painful to explain.

People self-harm for different reasons:

- To feel *something* when they're feeling numb
- To release pain that feels stuck inside
- To punish themselves when they feel worthless
- Because they think it's the only way to feel better

If that's something you've ever done, or even thought about—you are not alone. And more importantly, there are better ways to handle pain. Ways that don't hurt you.

One of the biggest lies your heavy thoughts will tell you is that you're too much—or not enough. That nobody would understand. That nobody would care. But here's the truth: people do care. People want to help. And healing is *always* possible—even if it takes time.

You might have thoughts that feel scary or confusing. Thoughts like, "I hate myself," or "I wish I could disappear." These thoughts don't make you bad. They mean you're overwhelmed. And when you're overwhelmed, the most powerful thing you can do is *talk*.

Not scream. Not act out. Just talk. Or write. Or create. Or reach out to someone who can hold your pain without judging you for it.

What Healing Looks Like

Healing doesn't happen all at once. It's not like flipping a light switch—it's more like slowly opening the blinds and letting a little more sunlight in each day. But that's OK

Sometimes healing looks like:

- Asking for help, even if your voice shakes
- Replacing self-harm with a new outlet (like journaling, music, or talking to a friend)
- Going to therapy, even if it feels awkward at first
- Getting enough sleep, drinking water, and moving your body

- Saying, "I'm not okay," and trusting someone to listen

You don't have to do it all today. Just one step at a time. That is the healthiest way to cope.

If you've ever felt like hurting yourself to deal with pain, here are some safer ways to express what you're feeling. These aren't magical fixes, but they can help interrupt the cycle.

Try one—or try them all:

- Hold an ice cube in your hand until it melts
- Rip paper into tiny pieces
- Scribble hard with a pencil until the page is black
- Run. Dance. Do jumping jacks. Move that energy out
- Listen to a playlist that matches your mood, or one that lifts it
- Write a letter you'll never send
- Talk to someone. Even if it's scary. Especially if it's scary.

And please—if you're feeling stuck in a cycle of hurting yourself, tell someone. A trusted adult. A school counselor. A hotline. Help is out there, and it *works*.

You Deserve Support!

If your leg was broken, you wouldn't try to just "walk it off." You'd go to the doctor. Get a cast. Rest and heal.

Mental health is the same. Just because the pain is invisible doesn't mean it isn't real.

You deserve:

- To be listened to
- To feel safe
- To not have to carry this alone
- To know that things can get better

Even if your home life is messy... Even if your friends don't get it... Even if you feel like you're drowning in silence... You still deserve help.

You are so much more than what you're going through. You are not your anxiety. You are not your depression. You are not your mistakes.

You are not what someone said about you. You are not your worst day.

You are a full human being—creative, funny, smart, sensitive, strong. You might be carrying some heavy stuff right now, but that doesn't define you.

Every sunrise is another chance to rewrite the story.

For the one who's reading this in silence, I see you. Even if you've never told anyone what you're going through. Even if you've hidden your feelings so deep you've forgotten where you left them. Even if your smile is a mask you wear to survive the day.

You are not invisible. You are not unlovable. You are not hopeless.

If no one has said it to you yet today, let me be the first:

I'm glad you're here.

So, breathe! Before we end this chapter, let's try something simple. Just take a moment to sit still. Put your hand on your heart and breathe in slowly for four seconds. Hold it. Breathe out for four more seconds. Do it again.

This small act of breathing with intention is a way to tell your brain: I'm here. I'm alive. And I'm trying.

That matters. That counts. And that's a powerful beginning.

Mental health journeys aren't straight lines. They're filled with ups, downs, spirals, and loops. But the point isn't perfection—it's *progress*.

Keep showing up for yourself. Keep asking questions. Keep replacing pain with purpose. Keep learning how to love yourself—even the parts that feel messy.

You're already doing one of the hardest, bravest things: facing the truth and choosing to grow. And every time you choose healing over hurting… You are breaking the cycle.

OFF THE RECORD

Use these pages to write your private thoughts off the record, you don't have to share them with anyone if you don't want to!

Chapter 5: Teaching Others How to Treat You

"How people treat you is their choice. How you respond is yours."
— Anonymous

Let's be real for a second.

From the day you're born, people start shaping you. Your parents put you on sleep schedules that fit *their* life. You're taught how to walk, talk, sit still, raise your hand, say "please," and "thank you." You go to school and learn how to stand in a line, follow the rules, and fit in.

You're basically trained from the start to behave a certain way—sometimes for your safety, sure, but sometimes just to make things easier for the adults around you.

But here's what no one talks about enough: while *you're* being trained to fit into the world, the world is also learning from *you.*

That's right—people are learning how to treat you based on what *you* allow, what *you* speak up about, and what *you* stay silent about.

Let that sink in.

Even if you're only 14, you're already teaching people every day.

- If you always let someone copy your homework, they'll think it's okay to take advantage of you.
- If you laugh at someone's rude joke, they'll think you're cool with it.
- If you stay quiet when someone crosses a boundary, they'll think they can do it again.

- If you let someone treat you like trash without ever setting a limit, they'll believe they can keep doing it.

This isn't about blame. It's about power.

You have more of it than you think.

Ever heard of Simone Biles? Or Naomi Osaka?

If you haven't, take a second and look them up. These two women are absolute legends. Simone is one of the most decorated gymnasts in history—like, she's done moves so hard they literally named them after her. Naomi? She's a tennis superstar who beat some of the best in the world before she even turned 23.

But here's what's really powerful about them: both Simone and Naomi decided to *stop*.

Not forever—but for a moment.

They stepped away from major competitions—not because they weren't good enough (they were) or scared (they weren't), but because their mental health needed care.

They were tired. Mentally. Emotionally. Physically.

And instead of pushing through just to make other people happy, they listened to themselves.

And not everyone liked it.

Some folks on the internet flipped out. "They're quitters!" "They let their teams down!" "They should just toughen up!"

The thing is, people are always going to have opinions. Most of those people couldn't even land a cartwheel, let alone do a double backflip with a twist. But that didn't stop them from judging.

That's how it is when you start teaching people how to treat you differently.

You set boundaries, and some people won't like it. You say, "I need a break," and they say, "You're lazy." You stand up for yourself, and they say you're dramatic.

But guess what? That's not your problem.

Just like Simone and Naomi, you don't owe anyone an explanation for protecting your peace.

Boundaries Aren't Walls—They're Filters

There's a difference between cutting people off and setting boundaries.

Boundaries say: "I care about myself enough to not let you treat me any kind of way." "I'm not okay with this, and I need something different." "I deserve respect, and I'm not afraid to ask for it."

When you set a boundary, you're saying, "I matter." And that's powerful.

It doesn't mean you're mean. It means you're mature.

You don't need to yell or be aggressive. Boundaries can sound like:

- "Hey, I don't like being called that. Please don't do it again."

- "I'm not in the mood to talk right now. Can we catch up later?"
- "I need some space. It's not about you—it's about me taking care of myself."

Remember, people learn how to treat you based on your reactions. If someone disrespects you and you let it slide over and over, they'll think it's fine. But if you speak up—even once—you're sending a new message.

You're teaching them, "Hey, this isn't okay with me."

And if they care about you, they'll adjust. If they don't? That's information. Not everyone deserves a front-row seat in your life.

The people you keep close should lift you up, not weigh you down.

Simone Biles and Naomi Osaka showed a different kind of strength. Not the kind that wins medals—but the kind that says, "I matter enough to pause. To breathe. To take care of me."

You don't have to be a famous athlete for this to apply to you.

You can say:

- "No, I'm not okay today."
- "I need a break from this friendship."
- "I need help, and I'm not ashamed of that."
- "I'm going to make a different choice—even if it disappoints someone else."

That kind of strength? It's rare. But it's yours if you want it.

When You're Afraid to Speak Up

Sometimes, the hardest person to stand up to is someone close to you—a best friend, a boyfriend/girlfriend, a parent, a coach.

But remember: love isn't control. Respect isn't silence. And loyalty doesn't mean letting people hurt you.

You're not "too sensitive" for having feelings. You're not "too much" for setting limits. You're not "selfish" for putting yourself first sometimes.

You're just human. And you're learning to take care of yourself.

What If You've Already Let People Treat You Badly?

It's okay. You're not stuck in the past.

If you've allowed certain behavior in the past, that doesn't mean you have to accept it forever. You can change the rules of engagement. You can say, "I know I let this happen before, but it doesn't sit right with me now."

That's growth. And it's brave.

People might be confused at first. Some might get defensive. That's normal. But the people who really care about you? They'll get it. And if they don't? That's their choice. Your job is to choose *you*.

This world will try to train you to believe all kinds of things, but you can rewrite the rules:

- That you should always say "yes" to please people
- That being "liked" matters more than being respected
- That working yourself to exhaustion is a badge of honor
- That you have to keep everyone happy to be worth something

Forget all that. Write your own rulebook. Start with this:

- I am allowed to rest.
- I am allowed to say no.
- I am allowed to take up space.
- I am allowed to be respected.

- I am allowed to change.
- I am allowed to be more than what others expect.

You're not here to make everyone comfortable. You're here to live a life that feels true to you.

OFF THE RECORD

Use these pages to write your private thoughts off the record, you don't have to share them with anyone if you don't want to!

Chapter 6 - The Definition of Family

Have you ever seen the movie *Soul Food*? It was written by Kenny "Babyface" Edmonds and centers around a woman named Big Mama—Mama Jo—who kept her family together through love, tradition, and her famous Sunday dinners. But everything changed when Big Mama passed away. The family fell apart. Arguments broke out. Secrets spilled. Money got involved, and suddenly, everyone was more focused on their own issues than on each other.

It was painful to watch—but also familiar.

In the movie, they eventually come back together. They forgive each other. They start doing the Sunday dinners again. It ends on a happy, feel-good note. And while it's beautiful to believe in healing like that, we all know real life doesn't always work that way. Sometimes, family problems don't get wrapped up with a bow. Sometimes, people don't apologize. Sometimes, the ones you thought would never walk away from you... do.

Every family has problems. Rich families. Poor families. Black families. White families. It doesn't matter where you come from or what your last name is. Drama doesn't discriminate. Some families put it all out in the open. Others hide it behind fake smiles and carefully planned holiday pictures. Some issues are loud and messy. Others are silent and heavy, just sitting there in the background, ignored.

I grew up in a family that had its own share of broken pieces. Still, my mom raised me to believe in the importance of family. I wanted something like what I saw on the *Cosby Show*—that picture-perfect family full of laughter, love, and togetherness. But the reality didn't match the dream.

It hurts when your idea of family doesn't line up with your actual experience. It hurts when people you're related to by blood feel more like strangers—or worse, enemies. And I know I'm not the only one who feels that way. I've talked to so many people who've opened up about what their families are really like. It turns out, a lot of us are walking around with the same questions, the same pain, the same confusion.

And it gets worse when someone dies. For some reason, family secrets tend to explode after a loss. People start acting different. Old arguments resurface. Everyone's emotions are high. Sometimes, you expect a death to bring people together, but instead, it rips everyone further apart. It's like everything people were hiding gets exposed at once, and nobody knows how to handle it.

The hardest part is when you don't understand why your family acts the way they do. Why is your uncle always angry? Why does your cousin never show up? Why is your mom so quick to shut down when things get emotional? When families don't talk about the past—about trauma, hurt feelings, or what really happened back then—you grow up confused about how people became the way they are. It's like walking into the middle of a movie with no idea what the first half was about.

I've been that person who didn't get the full story. And I've also been the person others misunderstood. I've assumed things about people that weren't true. And I've had people make assumptions about me. It's easy to point fingers—but sometimes those fingers need to be pointed at ourselves, too.

A lot of families fall apart not because of one big argument, but because of a bunch of little misunderstandings that add up over time. Someone gets hurt but never says anything. Someone else hears a rumor and believes it.

Someone makes a mistake and no one lets it go. Add in jealousy, gossip, or people outside the family stirring the pot, and suddenly the bond you thought was unbreakable starts falling apart.

And it's sad, because sometimes things *could* be fixed. Sometimes all it would take is one honest conversation, or a little more empathy. But not everything can be solved. Not everyone is willing to talk things out or meet you halfway. Life isn't like a movie. There's not always a happy ending.

But that doesn't mean there isn't hope.

Here's what I've learned: family isn't always about blood. Yes, your biological relatives are *a* kind of family. But sometimes, the people who show up for you the most—the ones who really see you and love you—aren't the ones you're related to. They might be your best friend. A teacher. A coach. A neighbor. Someone who checks in when you're having a bad day. Someone who listens and doesn't judge.

Those people? They're family, too.

And guess what? You get to decide who your real family is. Just because someone shares your last name doesn't mean they get to treat you badly. Just because someone is "supposed to" be there for you doesn't mean they automatically earn your trust. You get to protect your space. You get to choose who has access to your heart.

Family doesn't have to be perfect. It just has to be honest. Loving. Safe. And mutual.

So if you're sitting there wondering why your family feels distant… or why you feel more connected to your friends than to your cousins or siblings… or why you sometimes feel guilty for not wanting to be around certain relatives… take a deep breath. You're not weird. You're not dramatic. You're just growing.

You're learning to tell the difference between people who are connected to you… and people who show up for you. That's not betrayal. That's discernment. And it's one of the most important things you'll ever learn.

Real family is not just who raised you, or who shares your DNA. It's who sees you, values you, and helps you become your best self.

And that kind of family? You can build it. One connection at a time.

OFF THE RECORD

Use these pages to write your private thoughts off the record, you don't have to share them with anyone if you don't want to!

Chapter 7: Breaking the Cycle

There comes a moment—quiet, personal, and powerful—when you realize something has to change. Not because someone told you to, or because you're tired of hearing people complain. But because deep down, something inside you whispers, "You deserve better than this."

That moment is where the cycle starts to break.

For a long time, I thought healing meant fixing everyone else. If only my family could just get along. If only people would stop hurting each other. If only things were different. But eventually, I learned the truth:

you can't change the world around you until you start working on the world inside you.

And no one can do that for you.

People might cheer you on. They might wish you well. But healing only works if *you* want it. It starts with deciding that your past doesn't get to control your future. It starts with choosing to show up for yourself, even when it's hard.

Especially when it's hard.

When I first started thinking seriously about breaking my own cycles—the patterns that had followed me from childhood into my adult life—it was uncomfortable. Not dramatic. Just quiet and painful. I started hearing familiar things from different people: "You always assume the worst." "You don't let anyone help you." "You shut down when things get real." At first, I wanted to defend myself. I wanted to say, "Well, you would too if you'd been through what I have."

But then I realized… maybe they weren't attacking me. Maybe they were noticing something I couldn't see. Maybe the patterns I was repeating were connected to pain I'd never dealt with.

So I started asking myself real questions.

Why do I get angry so fast? Why do I trust people who don't treat me right? Why do I feel like I have to prove I'm worthy of love? Why do I carry so much and ask for so little?

And more importantly—where did I learn this?

It's wild how much we carry without realizing it. Some things aren't even ours. Maybe your mom or dad didn't know how to love without yelling. Maybe someone taught you that showing emotions was weak. Maybe no one ever told you that you were enough exactly as you are.

Sometimes, what we think is just "our personality" is actually just old pain dressed in new clothes.

That's what generational trauma is. It's the pain that keeps getting passed down—not always through words, but through habits, beliefs, silence. It's the rage we inherit. The fear. The guilt. The perfectionism. The people-pleasing. The shame. And until someone decides to stop and say, "No more," it keeps going. From one person to the next. Like a story stuck on repeat.

But it doesn't have to be that way.

You can be the one who rewrites the ending.

You can be the one who says, "I want to learn better ways to love." "I want to unlearn the lies I believed about myself." "I want to heal so that my future doesn't look like my past."

You don't need permission to become a better version of yourself. You don't need anyone to validate your growth. You just need to begin.

Start by looking at your own patterns, without shame. Think about how you react in certain situations. When you feel triggered or rejected or ignored—what do you do? What's your go-to move? Do you shut down? Do you lash out? Do you run away? Do you try to be perfect?

And then ask yourself: where did I learn this? Is this *me*, or is this something I picked up to survive?

Understanding yourself isn't about blaming your parents or tearing people down. It's about seeing clearly. If someone never gave you the love you needed, it's okay to admit that. If you were raised around yelling and chaos and now find yourself tense even in silence—that's valid. It doesn't make you broken. It means you're human.

Healing begins with honesty.

And sometimes that honesty will hurt.

But the good news is: pain doesn't mean you're failing. It means you're finally paying attention.

One of the hardest things to accept is that some people will not grow with you. Some people will stay stuck in their old ways. Some family members might not ever apologize. Some friends may not understand why you're changing. They may call you "different," "fake," or "distant."

That's okay.

Let them.

Your job isn't to make everyone else comfortable. Your job is to become the version of yourself you were always meant to be.

And part of that journey means learning to set boundaries. Learning to protect your peace. Learning to say "no" when something doesn't feel right. And "yes" when it does—even if no one else gets it.

There will be days when healing feels lonely. When it feels like you're carrying the weight of your entire family on your back. When you want to give up and fall back into old habits. When it feels like it's just too much.

Keep going.

You are not here to be perfect. You are here to grow. To change. To learn.

Breaking the cycle isn't about fixing everything overnight. It's about choosing, again and again, to do things differently.

To pause before reacting. To ask for help instead of staying silent. To forgive—not to forget, but to free yourself. To speak up. To rest. To try again.

It's about becoming the kind of person your younger self needed. And the kind of person your future self will be proud of.

No one is born knowing how to heal. No one gets it right all the time. But every time you choose growth over fear, love over resentment, and truth over denial—you're doing the work.

You're breaking the cycle.

And one day, someone else will look at you and say, "Because of you, I know I don't have to stay stuck."

Because of you, someone else will believe healing is possible.

And maybe—just maybe—that someone will be *you.*

OFF THE RECORD

Use these pages to write your private thoughts off the record, you don't have to share them with anyone if you don't want to!

Bonus Chapter: Giving What You Want to Receive

Sometimes, the best way to heal is to give the very thing you're missing. If you're looking for love, try giving love. If you want kindness, be kind. If you're craving respect, start by respecting others—and yourself. If you want to be heard, listen. If you're feeling invisible, make someone else feel seen.

It might sound backwards at first, especially if you're the one who's been hurt. You might be thinking, "Why should *I* be the one giving, when I've barely gotten anything from anyone?"

That's a valid question. But here's the thing: waiting around for someone else to fix you, love you, or save you? That can take forever. And in the meantime, you're missing your chance to take back your power.

Giving what you want to receive isn't about pretending you're okay when you're not. It's not about being fake or putting on a smile when you're falling apart inside. It's about *choosing* to create the energy you wish was around you.

You become what you practice. And the more you give something out, the more it starts to grow inside of you.

Don't misunderstand: you can't carry someone else's life on your shoulders. I am just talking about a small act of kindness. Just one small thing.

Think about a time when someone gave you a genuine compliment. It probably stayed with you longer than you expected. Maybe you were having a rough day, and someone said, "I like your hair," or "You're really good at that," and suddenly… things felt lighter. That one little moment didn't solve everything, but it changed *something*.

Now imagine being that moment for someone else.

You never know who's having a bad day. You never know who feels alone or unheard or like they're just barely holding it together. A simple word, a kind gesture, a little encouragement—it might seem small to you, but to someone else, it could mean everything.

And here's the coolest part: when you give that kind of love away, some of it always comes back. Not always from the same people. Not always right away. But it *always* comes back.

When I started working on myself, I realized I'd spent a lot of time waiting. Waiting for apologies I never got. Waiting for people to notice me. Waiting for someone to say, "You matter." But the more I waited, the emptier I felt.

One day, I just got tired. Not in a sad way—in a strong way. I got tired of waiting and decided I was going to *become* the kind of person I'd always wished I had in my corner.

I started giving compliments, even when I wasn't feeling confident. I reached out to friends, even when I was the one who needed someone to check in. I forgave people—not because they said sorry, but because *I* needed peace.

And little by little, I started to feel lighter. Not perfect. Not fully healed. But stronger.

This isn't about being a doormat or ignoring your own needs. It's about flipping the script.

If you feel like no one understands you, try understanding someone else. If you've been hurt, be gentle—with yourself and others. If you've made mistakes, offer grace—to yourself and others.

Giving is powerful. It reminds you that you are *not* helpless. You're not just a product of your past—you're a builder of your future.

And when you give the things you've been missing, you start to become the person *you* needed. You become someone you can be proud of.

Healing doesn't always look like deep conversations or therapy sessions or journaling (although those things help too). Sometimes, healing looks like laughing with someone who needs it. Sometimes it looks like holding the door open for a stranger, texting someone a meme, or choosing not to say something mean when you're hurt.

Every small act of love is a brick in the house you're building for yourself. A safe house. A strong house. A home in your heart that no one can take from you.

You are not stuck.

You don't have to wait to feel better before you start spreading good energy. You don't have to be all the way healed to start helping others heal.

Start now.

Be kind when you can. Be generous with your encouragement. Be open to giving love, even if you're still figuring out how to receive it.

And give yourself some of that same energy too.

You deserve your own kindness. You deserve your own patience. You deserve to be loved—even if you're still a work in progress. Especially then.

You are someone's safe space. You are someone's moment of hope. You are someone's "I needed that today." You are proof that love is still out here—even in a world that sometimes feels cold.

So go ahead. Give what you want to receive.

And in doing that, you just might find… you've had it inside you all along.

OFF THE RECORD

Use these pages to write your private thoughts off the record, you don't have to share them with anyone if you don't want to!

OFF THE RECORD

Use these pages to write your private thoughts off the record, you don't have to share them with anyone if you don't want to!

OFF THE RECORD

Use these pages to write your private thoughts off the record, you don't have to share them with anyone if you don't want to!

OFF THE RECORD

Use these pages to write your private thoughts off the record, you don't have to share them with anyone if you don't want to!

OFF THE RECORD

Use these pages to write your private thoughts off the record, you don't have to share them with anyone if you don't want to!

OFF THE RECORD

Use these pages to write your private thoughts off the record, you don't have to share them with anyone if you don't want to!

OFF THE RECORD

Use these pages to write your private thoughts off the record, you don't have to share them with anyone if you don't want to!

OFF THE RECORD

Use these pages to write your private thoughts off the record, you don't have to share them with anyone if you don't want to!

OFF THE RECORD

Use these pages to write your private thoughts off the record, you don't have to share them with anyone if you don't want to!

OFF THE RECORD

Use these pages to write your private thoughts off the record, you don't have to share them with anyone if you don't want to!

OFF THE RECORD

Use these pages to write your private thoughts off the record, you don't have to share them with anyone if you don't want to!

OFF THE RECORD

Use these pages to write your private thoughts off the record, you don't have to share them with anyone if you don't want to!

OFF THE RECORD

Use these pages to write your private thoughts off the record, you don't have to share them with anyone if you don't want to!

OFF THE RECORD

Use these pages to write your private thoughts off the record, you don't have to share them with anyone if you don't want to!

About the Author

Chlarissa, a devoted wife and mother, is deeply engaged in community service. A former teen mom, she mentored others through the Birthing Project in Little Rock, AR, and founded D2NINE to empower African American women. She has also mentored young girls via Big Brothers/Big Sisters of Central Arkansas. A member of Alpha Kappa Alpha Sorority, Inc. and the Order of the Eastern Star, she has organized empowerment conferences supporting women and alienated fathers. In her free time, she enjoys traveling and beachside relaxation, advocating for global healing and self-discovery.

REVIEWS MATTER

If you enjoyed this book, please help others find it by leaving a review on the site where you purchased it. Thank you for your support.

www.ingramcontent.com/pod-product-compliance
Lightning Source LLC
Chambersburg PA
CBHW071331130626
46556CB00004B/1847